MAHLIA AMATINA

The Autistic Employee Workplace Toolkit

First edition

ISBN: 978-1-9195538-8-7

Editing by Grace Gilbert
Cover art by Erin Caitlin Karn (using licensed Canva elements)

This book was professionally typeset on Reedsy.
Find out more at reedsy.com

Contents

Introduction

Dear Reader,

I wrote this book for you.

Not the "you" that the world sometimes demands; the polished, endlessly adaptable, always-on professional. I mean the real you: autistic, navigating a world that wasn't built with our brains in mind, figuring out how to show up every day in workplaces that often prize conformity over authenticity.

When I was first starting out in the world of work, I didn't have a guidebook. I learned through trial and error, often painfully. There were jobs where I felt valued and understood, and others where I left at the end of each day with my shoulders hunched, my head pounding and my self-esteem chipped away. There were times I masked so hard, hiding my natural communication style, suppressing stimming, forcing small talk, that I'd come home exhausted, my body aching from the effort.

It took me years to understand something simple yet radical:

Thriving at work isn't about "fixing" ourselves to fit in – it's about knowing ourselves, understanding our rights, and building environments that work for us.

Why This Toolkit Exists

Globally, autistic people face an employment crisis. The statistics are sobering:

- In the UK, only 29% of autistic adults are in any form of paid employment (Office for National Statistics, 2021).
- In the US, estimates range from 14% to 34%, depending on the definition of employment and the sample studied (National Autism Indicators Report, Drexel University, 2017).

Autistic people are more likely than any other disability group to be unemployed, yet when in the right environment, we often outperform expectations in productivity, attention to detail and creative problem-solving.

This toolkit is my attempt to fill a gap; to offer not just "how-to" advice, but also solidarity, compassion and validation. You deserve to feel seen and supported, not just "accommodated".

What Being Autistic at Work Means to Me

I'm autistic, and I see the world differently. I process information deeply, notice patterns others miss and can hyperfocus on meaningful projects for hours. These are strengths. But they come with challenges, like sensory overwhelm in noisy offices, the mental gymnastics of decoding unspoken workplace rules and the fatigue of navigating social expectations that aren't intuitive to me.

For me, thriving at work isn't about chasing promotions at all costs. It's about having the space to do my best work without burning out, being able to take a lunch break without masking through "team banter", and having my contributions valued as they are - not as they would be if I were more "typical".

When I speak to other autistic professionals, I hear the same themes:

- The relief of finding a manager who listens.
- The frustration of inaccessible hiring processes.

- The joy of working in an environment where stimming isn't policed.
- The exhaustion of constantly proving your worth.

This book is here to help you navigate those realities.

How to Use This Toolkit

Think of this book as a companion you can turn to at any stage of your working life:

- If you're starting a new job and want to lay a foundation for success.
- If you're struggling and need strategies to advocate for yourself or request adjustments.
- If you're planning your career path and want to build it on your terms.

Each chapter blends:

- Practical advice you can act on immediately.
- Real stories (including my own) to remind you you're not alone.
- Research and legal context so you know your rights and can challenge misconceptions.
- Reflection prompts to help you figure out what's right for you, not just what the workplace says is right.

You don't have to read in order. Start where you are; maybe disclosure is on your mind, or maybe you're grappling with burnout. Dip in, take what you need and come back when you're ready.

My Promise to You

I won't tell you to "just be yourself" without acknowledging that for many autistic people, being ourselves in the workplace can come at a cost. I won't sugarcoat the challenges, but I will remind you, again and again, that you have value, that you belong and that thriving at work is possible.

By the end of this book, I hope you'll feel:

- More confident in understanding your needs and rights.
- Better equipped to advocate for yourself.
- Inspired to shape your work life in a way that truly supports you.

Because your work matters, and so do you.

1

Understanding Yourself as an Autistic Employee

When I first entered the workplace, I thought success meant blending in. I tried to dress like everyone else, speak like everyone else, work like everyone else, even when that meant working against my natural rhythms. It was exhausting. Over time, I realised that understanding myself and how I function best as an autistic person was the single most important key to thriving at work.

This chapter is about that first step: getting to know yourself as an autistic employee so you can build your career around your strengths, navigate your challenges and meet your needs without apology.

What Autism Means in the Context of Work

Autism is a form of neurodivergence; a natural variation in the way brains process information, communicate and interact with the world. In the workplace, this can translate into different communication styles, sensory preferences, approaches to problem-solving and ways of organising tasks.

For example:

- You might hyperfocus on projects you care about, producing exceptional results.
- You might be more comfortable with written communication than spontaneous meetings.
- You might notice patterns, details or risks others overlook.

But in a work culture built on neurotypical norms, these differences can be misunderstood. A preference for direct communication can be labelled as "bluntness". Avoiding the bustling staff kitchen might be seen as being "anti-social". These aren't flaws, they're simply differences.

Research Insight:

Did you know that autistic employees often show higher accuracy rates in data analysis, pattern recognition and quality control tasks than non-autistic peers (Austin & Pisano, Harvard Business Review, 2017)? Yet these skills are often overlooked because recruitment and promotion systems focus on social "fit" over capability.

Recognising Your Strengths and Challenges

One of the most empowering things you can do is take stock of your own strengths and challenges in the context of work.

When I did this exercise for myself, I realised my strengths included:

- Creative problem-solving.
- Deep focus on meaningful projects.
- Empathy for others' experiences.
- Strong written communication skills.

My challenges included:

- Navigating office politics.
- Managing unexpected changes to plans.
- Sensory overwhelm in bright, noisy environments.
- Sustaining small talk without fatigue.

Neither list was "good" or "bad"; it was simply *true*. Once I understood these patterns, I could make better decisions about the roles I took, the environments I worked in and the strategies I used to help myself.

Reflection Prompt:

Write down three strengths you bring to your work and three areas you find challenging. Be as specific as you can; "good at problem-solving" is fine, but "can quickly identify broken workflows and suggest improvements" is better.

Understanding Sensory Needs and Emotional Responses

Workplaces are sensory minefields: buzzing lights, overlapping conversations or the smell of reheated lunches. For some autistic people, these sensations are just mildly annoying, yet for others, they can cause genuine distress or even physical pain.

I once worked in an open-plan office with constant foot traffic behind my desk. My brain felt like it was on high alert all day, scanning for movement. I went home every night with a tension headache. It wasn't until I moved to a quieter corner that I realised how much energy I'd been spending simply to endure my environment.

Recognising your sensory triggers and the adjustments that help is key. This might mean:

- Wearing noise-cancelling headphones (or ordinary headphones)
- Adjusting lighting (or requesting a desk near a window)
- Taking regular sensory breaks
- Using remote work options to manage overload

Research Insight:

Sensory overload at work is a significant factor in autistic burnout, a state of physical and emotional exhaustion that can take months to recover from (Raymaker et al., *Autism in Adulthood*, 2020).

Embracing Neurodiversity: You Are Not Alone

When I began connecting with other autistic professionals, both in person and online, I realised how powerful it is to know you're not the only one navigating these experiences. Neurodiversity is a growing movement recognising that different brain types bring diverse strengths to society and work.

Research Insight:

Companies with diverse teams (including neurodivergent employees) are 36% more likely to outperform their peers in profitability (McKinsey & Co., 2020).

Community is not just about support; it's about strategy. Other autistic employees can share tips for handling interviews, scripts for requesting adjustments or simply reassurance that it's okay to work in your own way.

Key Takeaways from Chapter 1

- Understanding yourself is the foundation for thriving at work.
- Your strengths and challenges are information, not judgements.
- Sensory needs are valid and deserve to be addressed.
- You are part of a wider autistic community, with collective knowledge and resilience.

Reflection Questions

1. What are three strengths you want to lean into more at work?
2. What are three challenges you'd like to manage differently?
3. What sensory adjustments might improve your work environment?
4. Who in your network can you connect with for shared understanding and advice?

2

Navigating Disclosure - Your Choices and Rights

Disclosure is one of the most personal, and sometimes most complicated, decisions you can make at work. It's the moment you decide whether, when and how to tell your employer, colleagues or HR that you are autistic.

For some, disclosure is freeing. It can open the door to understanding, adjustments and a sense of authenticity. For others, it can be a source of anxiety, with worries about prejudice, stereotyping or career impact. There's no "right" answer, only what's right for you in your given situation.

The Reality of Disclosure

According to a 2020 survey by the National Autistic Society, over 50% of autistic employees have chosen *not* to disclose their diagnosis at work, often due to fear of discrimination or misunderstanding. Unfortunately, these fears aren't unfounded: research from Great Britain's Equality and Human Rights Commission has found that disabled employees still experience higher rates of workplace harassment and exclusion compared to their non-disabled peers.

I've personally experienced both sides of the coin. In one workplace, disclosure led to constructive conversations and helpful adjustments: flexible hours, noise-reducing headphones and a manager who genuinely wanted to understand. In another, my openness was met with polite nods but no real change, and sometimes subtle signals that my differences were a "problem" to be managed.

This variability is why it's important to weigh your decision carefully.

Reasons You Might Choose to Disclose

- **Accessing reasonable adjustments**: In Great Britain, the Equality Act 2010 requires employers to make "reasonable adjustments" to support disabled employees who are experiencing long-term negative effects daily, including those who are autistic. This could mean changes to your workspace, flexible hours or communication styles. But to access these, it often helps to explain your needs, and sometimes your diagnosis.
- **Building understanding**: Disclosure can help colleagues understand behaviours they might otherwise misinterpret, like avoiding eye contact, preferring written communication or needing a quiet space.
- **Being authentic**: For some people, hiding autism at work is exhausting. Disclosure can lift the mental load and strain of masking.
- **Challenging stereotypes**: Sharing your experience can educate others and contribute to a more inclusive culture (although this is emotional labour, and it's not your responsibility alone).

Reasons You Might Choose Not to disclose

- **Concerns about discrimination**: Even with legal protections, bias still exists. Some employers may unconsciously (or consciously) view autism through a deficit lens.
- **Privacy**: Your diagnosis is personal information. You may prefer to keep it separate from your professional life.
- **Testing the waters first**: You might want to observe your workplace culture before making a decision.
- **Focusing on adjustments, not labels**: You can request changes based on needs rather than diagnosis (e.g., "I work best in a quieter space") without using the term "autism".

How to Decide: A Step-By-Step Approach

1 - Assess your workplace culture

- Is there evidence of inclusion? Are managers supportive of other employees with different needs?
- What's the HR process for requesting adjustments?

2 - Know your legal rights

- In Great Britain, you are protected under the Equality Act 2010 from discrimination based on disability. Autism is recognised as a disability if it has a substantial, long-term impact on your ability to carry out day-to-day activities, which includes workplace tasks.

3 - Consider timing

- You can disclose at any stage: during recruitment, after an offer or

months/years into a job.
- Some people choose to wait until they've established themselves in a role.

4 - Plan your message

- Decide how much detail to share; you don't need to give your full medical history.
- Focus on strengths as well as needs: "My attention to detail helps me excel in X, and I do my best work when...".

5 - Choose your audience

- Disclosure doesn't have to be all-or-nothing. You can tell your manager but not your colleagues, or share with HR, but not your direct supervisor.

Real-Life Example: "Sarah's story"

Sarah, a marketing executive in her late twenties, was diagnosed autistic at 25. She decided to disclose to her manager after realising that back-to-back meetings were leaving her overwhelmed. Her disclosure was framed around solutions:

"I've recently learned I'm autistic, which helps me understand my working style better. To do my best work, I need short breaks between meetings to process and refocus."

Her manager was receptive, and together they restructured her schedule. Six months later, Sarah reported feeling more energised and productive.

Research Insight:

A 2024 Harvard Business Review article by Ludmila N. Praslova, "How to Weigh the Risks of Disclosing a Disability," highlights the complex dynamics of workplace disclosure for individuals with conditions such as neurodivergence. The article emphasises that disclosure can unlock access to accommodations and foster inclusion, but only when met with understanding and action. Conversely, when disclosure is met with scepticism, dismissal or inaction, trust in the organisation can deteriorate sharply, and employees may experience increased burnout and disengagement.

If Things Go Wrong

If disclosure leads to discrimination or inaction:

- Document all interactions (emails, meeting notes).
- Seek advice from your HR department, union or an organisation like ACAS (in Great Britain).
- Know that you have legal options under the Equality Act 2010, but weigh the emotional cost of pursuing them.

Reflection Questions

1. What's your gut feeling about disclosure in your current (or prospective) workplace?
2. If you were to disclose, who would you feel most comfortable telling first, and why?
3. What adjustments would you request, with or without disclosure?
4. How would you frame your strengths alongside your needs in a disclosure conversation?

3

Self-Advocacy at Work

Self-advocacy means speaking up for yourself, your needs and your rights. It's about understanding what works best for you and communicating that clearly at work. For autistic employees, self-advocacy is not just a useful skill; it's often essential for thriving in environments that may not naturally accommodate our ways of thinking and processing.

I remember when I first started to self-advocate at work. It was scary. I worried I'd be seen as "difficult" or "complaining". But over time, I learned that advocating for myself was the key to building trust, gaining respect and creating a workspace where I could be my authentic self.

Research supports this: a 2023 study published in the *Journal of Autism and Developmental Disorders* found that autistic employees who experience autonomy and are able to advocate for their needs report greater work motivation and satisfaction. Drawing on Self-Determination Theory, the study emphasises that being able to ask for adjustments or explain how you work best not only reduces stress and burnout, but also enhances engagement, wellbeing and a sense of purpose in the workplace. The authors highlight that motivation is not a fixed trait; it can be cultivated through supportive environments that meet psychological needs for autonomy, competence and relatedness

(Goldfarb, Golan, & Gal, 2023).

Defining Key Terms

- **Self-advocacy**: The action of representing and defending your own interests, needs and rights.
- **Reasonable Adjustments**: Changes or accommodations made by an employer to support an employee with disabilities, such as autism.
- **Intersectionality**: The way different aspects of a person's identity (like race, gender, neurodivergence) combine to create unique experiences of discrimination or privilege. For example, being autistic *and* from a minority ethnic background can impact how you experience workplace inclusion.

Why Self-Advocacy Matters for Autistic Employees

Autistic employees often face unique challenges that others may not notice or understand. Sensory sensitivities, communication differences and social interaction styles can all affect how we navigate the workplace. Self-advocacy lets us explain these challenges in a way that builds understanding rather than stigma.

Consider this: the *Office for National Statistics* data shows that around 3 in 10 working-age autistic adults in the UK were in employment in 2021. One major reason is the lack of appropriate support and understanding from employers. Self-advocacy can bridge this gap by helping us express what we need to succeed.

Real-Life Example: My Experience with Self-Advocacy

I remember a job when I struggled with the open-plan office environment. The constant noise and movement made it hard to concentrate, and I often felt overwhelmed. I was hesitant to say anything at first, fearing judgment. But when I finally spoke to my manager, explaining my sensory needs and suggesting simple adjustments like wearing headphones and occasional quiet workspace access, things improved dramatically. Not only did my productivity increase, but my confidence grew because I felt seen and supported.

How to Build Your Self-Advocacy Skills

1. **Know Your Needs** Start by identifying what helps you do your best work. Is it written instructions instead of verbal? Regular breaks? Flexible hours? Being clear about your needs is the foundation of self-advocacy.
2. **Learn Your Rights** Understanding your legal rights around workplace adjustments and disability protections empowers you. In Great Britain, the Equality Act 2010 requires employers to make reasonable adjustments for disabled employees, including those with autism.
3. **Prepare Your Message** Think about how to communicate your needs clearly and calmly. Use "I" statements, e.g., "I find it easier to focus when I have a quiet workspace".
4. **Choose the Right Time and Person** Sometimes it helps to schedule a meeting with your manager or HR, so you have their full attention.
5. **Practice Self-Compassion** Self-advocacy can be exhausting and emotionally challenging. Be kind to yourself and celebrate small wins.

Case Study: Self-Advocacy in Action

Liam, an autistic software developer, found it difficult to ask for adjustments. After attending a self-advocacy workshop, he wrote a clear email to his manager explaining his need for flexible working hours and a noise-reduced workspace. His manager responded positively and arranged adjustments that helped Liam not only stay in his role but also earn a promotion within two years.

Overcoming Barriers to Self-Advocacy

Barriers like fear of stigma, previous negative experiences or misunderstanding your own needs can make self-advocacy hard. Here are some tips:

- **Build a Support Network:** Allies at work, mentors or external autism support groups can boost your confidence.
- **Use Written Communication:** Sometimes writing your needs down helps avoid pressure in face-to-face conversations.
- **Take Small Steps:** Start with minor requests and gradually build up to bigger conversations.
- **Know It's Okay to Say No:** You don't have to accept unreasonable requests or environments that harm your wellbeing.

Self-advocacy is a journey, not a destination. Each time you speak up, you strengthen your voice and build a workplace where you can truly flourish. Remember, your needs are valid, and by advocating for yourself you're helping to create a better environment not just for you, but for other autistic colleagues too.

Reflection Questions

1. What are three things you know help you work well? How comfortable are you expressing these at work?
2. What fears or concerns do you have about self-advocacy? What might help you overcome them?
3. Who at work do you trust or feel could support you in advocating for your needs?
4. How can you prepare for a conversation about your workplace needs or adjustments?
5. What small step can you take this week to practice self-advocacy?

4

Requesting and Using Reasonable Adjustments

What Are Reasonable Adjustments?

Reasonable adjustments (sometimes called accommodations) are changes or support your employer makes to help you do your job effectively. These adjustments are meant to reduce barriers that might arise because of autism and/or other conditions.

For example, this might include flexible working hours, a quieter workspace, modified communication methods or extra time for tasks. The goal is to level the playing field so that you can perform at your best.

Under the Equality Act 2010, employers have a legal duty to provide reasonable adjustments to disabled employees who are struggling daily with long term problems, and autism is recognised as a disability under this law.

Research Insight:

Davies et al. (2022) found that when autistic employees must shoulder the burden of identifying and requesting workplace adjustments, and face barriers to getting them, this shortfall undermines their wellbeing and influences their career choices. Participants emphasised that employer-led, proactive adjustment processes are crucial for sustaining job satisfaction and reducing stress.

Why Reasonable Adjustments Matter

Many autistic employees don't receive the adjustments they need, often because they don't know what to ask for or they fear stigma. According to a 2023 report by the *Centre for Inclusive Employment*, over 50% of autistic workers said they had never asked for adjustments, even though many experienced significant challenges.

But reasonable adjustments can make a huge difference. I've personally found that with the right adjustments in place, I can reduce sensory overload, manage my energy better, communicate more effectively and just generally get on better. And these changes don't just benefit me; they improve team productivity and morale too.

Common Reasonable Adjustments for Autistic Employees

Here are some examples of adjustments you might consider asking for:

- **Sensory adjustments:** Noise-cancelling headphones, desk placement away from busy areas, control over lighting.
- **Flexible working:** Adjusted start and finish times, the option to work from home.
- **Communication preferences:** Receiving instructions in writing, having agendas before meetings, using email instead of phone calls.
- **Task management:** Breaking projects into smaller steps, extra time for deadlines, priority lists.
- **Social support:** A mentor or buddy, clear workplace policies, training for colleagues about autism.

How to Request Reasonable Adjustments

Requesting adjustments can feel intimidating, especially if you worry about being misunderstood or rejected. Here's a step-by-step approach that worked well for me:

1. **Prepare**: Write down the specific challenges you face and what adjustments you believe would help. Use clear, simple language and be ready to explain how the adjustments will improve your work.
2. **Know Your Rights**: Familiarise yourself with your company's policies and the legal framework, like the Equality Act 2010. Knowing that you are supported by law can boost your confidence.
3. **Choose Your Approach**: You might want to speak directly to your line manager, HR or occupational health services. Some people prefer to start with an email to create a clear record.
4. **Be Open and Collaborative**: Present your request as a way to help you contribute your best work, not as a complaint. For example, say, "I've noticed I work best when I have quieter surroundings, and I think having a desk away from the main office area would really help".
5. **Follow Up**: If adjustments are agreed, make sure they're implemented and check in regularly to discuss how well they're working.

Real-Life Example: Getting the Right Adjustment for Me

Early in my diagnosis journey, I felt overwhelmed by unexpected changes in my schedule. I requested a reasonable adjustment to have my weekly timetable confirmed in advance and to receive any changes by email at least 24 hours ahead. This simple adjustment reduced my anxiety enormously and helped me plan my sensory and social energy.

Using Adjustments Effectively

Once you have adjustments in place, it's important to use them proactively. Here are some tips:

- **Be consistent**: Use your adjustments regularly to make them a natural part of your work routine.
- **Communicate openly**: If something isn't working, speak up. Adjustments can be tweaked as needed.
- **Educate your team**: Sometimes colleagues don't understand why adjustments are necessary. Sharing information (with your permission) can build empathy.
- **Monitor your wellbeing**: Keep track of how adjustments impact your stress, focus and job satisfaction.

Overcoming Common Challenges

Sometimes employers resist making adjustments due to misunderstandings or budget concerns. Remember:

- Adjustments don't have to be expensive or complex.
- Employers can seek advice from occupational health or external experts.
- You can ask for a phased or trial period to show the benefits.

If you encounter resistance, consider seeking advice from disability employment services, unions or autism support organisations.

Reasonable adjustments aren't special favours; they are your right and a practical way to create a workplace that values diverse strengths. Remember, asking for what you need shows strength, not weakness.

Reflection Questions

1. What adjustments do you think would help you perform your best at work?
2. Have you ever requested adjustments before? If yes, how did it go? If no, what stopped you?
3. Who in your workplace could support you in requesting or implementing adjustments?
4. How can you communicate your needs in a clear and positive way?
5. What will you do if your request for adjustments isn't immediately accepted?

5

Managing Sensory Overload and Emotional Wellbeing

Sensory overload is one of the most common and challenging experiences for autistic people in the workplace. It happens when the brain receives more sensory input than it can process comfortably. This overload can come from many sources: bright or flickering lights, loud or unpredictable noises, strong smells, crowded spaces or even the tactile feel of certain clothing or furniture.

For me, it was the constant fluorescent lighting and the open-plan office chatter that built up over the day until I felt like my brain was on fire. This isn't just discomfort; sensory overload can cause physical pain, anxiety and exhaustion, making it hard or impossible to focus or stay calm.

Why Sensory Overload Matters at Work

A 2021 study in *Autism Research* found that sensory overload is a near-universal experience among autistic adults, with direct links to workplace stress, emotional wellbeing, and job retention (MacLennan et al., 2021). Sensory overload can affect not just performance but also emotional wellbeing and job retention.

This is why managing sensory environments and our emotional responses to them is crucial, not a luxury or "nice to have", but a key to thriving at work.

The Emotional Toll of Masking and Overwhelm

Beyond sensory input, many of us carry the weight of "masking": the exhausting process of hiding or suppressing our natural behaviours, reactions and needs to fit in socially. While masking can help us navigate social expectations, it comes at a steep emotional cost.

Pearson and Rose (2021) argue that autistic masking is linked with elevated anxiety and depression, and can contribute to profound emotional exhaustion. I have lived with this firsthand. For years, I tried to appear "neurotypical" at work, suppressing stimming behaviours and forcing consistent eye contact. The effort drained me emotionally, leaving me feeling isolated and misunderstood.

Emotional Wellbeing Is Part of Sensory Management

Managing emotional wellbeing means recognising how sensory overload and masking affect your feelings, and how to actively care for your mental health. This holistic approach helps you not just survive your workday, but also feel more balanced and empowered.

Practical Strategies to Manage Sensory Overload

Here are the strategies I've found most helpful, drawn from my own experience and supported by research:

1 - Create a Sensory-Friendly Workspace

Use noise-cancelling headphones or earplugs to reduce auditory overload. Noise-cancelling devices can significantly improve concentration and reduce stress for autistic employees.

Request a desk away from high-traffic or noisy areas if possible.

Control lighting: ask for lamps instead of harsh overhead lights or use natural light where you can.

Personalise your space with calming colours, textures or objects that soothe you.

2 - Schedule Sensory Breaks

Regular breaks give your nervous system a chance to reset. Even a few minutes spent outside, walking or doing deep breathing can help reduce overload.

I set alarms on my phone to remind myself to take sensory breaks every 90 minutes. These breaks are non-negotiable; without them, I spiral into overwhelm.

3 - Use Grounding Techniques

Grounding exercises help bring your attention back to the present moment when sensory overload triggers panic or shutdown.

Examples include:

- Focusing on your breath.
- Naming five things you can see, four you can touch, three you can hear.
- Holding a comforting object, like a smooth stone or a stress ball.

4 - Prepare for Sensory Challenges

When you know you'll face a potentially overwhelming event, like a busy meeting or noisy commute, plan ahead. Bring headphones, arrange quieter routes or negotiate flexible working hours.

5 - Practice Self-Compassion

Remember that sensory overload isn't a sign of weakness or failure. It's a natural reaction of your nervous system. Be gentle with yourself when you need to step away or ask for help.

Managing Emotional Wellbeing

Your emotional health is just as important as managing sensory inputs. Here's how I nurture my emotional wellbeing:

1. Recognise and Validate Your Feelings

Your emotions are valid, even when they don't fit neurotypical norms. Allow yourself to feel frustration, anxiety or exhaustion without judgment.

2. Seek Support When Needed

Therapy or coaching with professionals experienced in autism can be invaluable. I've found working with a neurodivergent-affirming therapist helped me process work-related anxiety and build resilience.

Peer support groups and autism communities also offer safe spaces to share experiences and advice.

3. Build Routines That Support You

Routines provide predictability, reducing anxiety. Incorporate calming activities into your day, whether it's mindfulness, journalling, gentle exercise or hobbies.

4. Manage Energy, Not Just Time

Autistic people often experience "spoons" or limited energy reserves. Learning to manage energy, recognising when you're running low and taking restorative actions, is key to avoiding burnout.

5. Understand and Reduce Masking

Where safe, reduce the need for masking by:

- Being open with trusted colleagues about your autism.

- Creating environments where your natural behaviours are accepted.
- Advocating for neurodiversity training at work.

I've found that the less I mask, the more authentic and less exhausted I feel.

Personal Story: Overcoming Sensory Overload

Early in my career, I felt trapped by sensory overload. I remember one day when the office construction noise was unbearable, I felt panic rise and had no escape. After that, I asked for a quiet workspace and permission to take sensory breaks, which was met with understanding.

This small change transformed my work life. I could focus better, my anxiety levels dropped, and I felt more confident advocating for myself.

Managing sensory overload and emotional wellbeing is not a one-size-fits-all process. It requires listening to your body and mind, experimenting with strategies and asking for support when needed. By prioritising these areas, you're not only protecting yourself but setting the foundation to thrive and grow in your career.

Reflection Questions

1. What sensory triggers affect you most at work? How can you minimise them or manage their impact?
2. What early signs tell you that sensory overload is building? How can you respond quickly?
3. What grounding or calming techniques resonate with you? Can you try one this week?
4. How do you currently care for your emotional wellbeing? What new practices might support you?
5. In what ways might masking affect your wellbeing? What steps can

you take to reduce it safely?

6

Communicating Your Needs and Boundaries

Communicating our needs and boundaries at work is one of the most empowering things we can do as autistic employees. For me, it was a turning point once I learned to speak up clearly and kindly about what I needed. I noticed relationships improved, misunderstandings decreased, and my own stress dropped significantly.

Yet, communication can feel like a minefield. Many of us were taught to "blend in" by keeping our needs to ourselves, or we worry about being judged or rejected if we say too much. But here's the truth: your needs and boundaries are valid and sharing them helps create an environment where you can succeed.

What Are Boundaries?

Boundaries are limits you set around your energy, time and wellbeing. They help protect you from burnout, confusion or stress. Boundaries can be about anything, from how and when you communicate, to what social interactions you're comfortable with, to how much work you can realistically take on.

Setting boundaries isn't selfish. It's a vital act of self-care and professionalism.

Why Communication Can Be Challenging for Autistic People

Research shows that many autistic adults face barriers to effective communication in the workplace, due to differences in social styles, sensory sensitivities or past negative experiences (Petty et al., 2022).

For example, I often found it difficult to read between the lines or interpret implied messages. I sometimes worried that if I was too direct, I'd upset colleagues. These concerns can lead to avoidance, which leaves needs unmet and frustrations unspoken.

Learning to communicate in a way that feels authentic yet clear can transform these challenges.

My Journey to Clear Communication

In my early jobs, I often said "yes" to requests even when overwhelmed, and I didn't express when sensory inputs were too much. This led to exhaustion and feelings of resentment.

Gradually, I learned that:

- Preparing what I want to say helps me feel confident.
- Using "I" statements makes conversations less confrontational.
- Writing things down, whether in emails or notes, clarifies my needs.
- Sharing my communication preferences with colleagues and managers fosters understanding.

One memorable moment was when I told my manager, "I work best when instructions are given in writing before meetings," which made a huge difference to how I could prepare and participate.

Practical Steps to Communicate Your Needs and Boundaries

1. Identify Your Needs and Limits

Reflect on what you need to feel comfortable and productive. What drains your energy? What helps you prosper? Knowing this clearly is the first step to effective communication.

2. Choose Your Communication Style

You might prefer:

- Written communication: Emails, chat messages or notes.
- Verbal conversations: One-to-one meetings or phone calls.
- Visual aids: Diagrams or schedules.

Consider which method feels safest and clearest for you.

3. Prepare What to Say

Planning your words in advance reduces anxiety. Use clear, simple language and "I" statements:

"I find it helpful to have deadlines a week in advance."

"I feel overwhelmed by unexpected meetings and would appreciate notice."

4. Set Boundaries with Kindness and Firmness

It's okay to say no or ask for adjustments. For example:

"I'm currently at capacity with my tasks and won't be able to take on additional projects this week."

"I need to step away from social events early to manage my energy."

5. Practice Active Listening and Ask for Feedback

Communication is two-way. Check that your message was understood and be open to clarifying.

6. Seek Allies and Supports

If direct communication feels too daunting, consider:

- Having a trusted colleague or mentor advocate for you.
- Using HR or occupational health services as intermediaries.

Fear of Being Judged or Rejected

Many autistic people fear their needs will be seen as "too much." But research and personal stories show that clear communication actually builds respect and trust.

You get to decide how much personal information you share. You can explain your needs without disclosing your diagnosis, or you can choose to be open if you feel safe.

If someone reacts poorly, remind yourself it's their response, not your worth. I know it can be hard to separate the two. Seek support and consider formal channels if necessary.

Using Communication to Prevent Burnout

Clear communication and boundary-setting are powerful tools against burnout. By saying what you need and what's too much, you reduce overwhelm and maintain energy.

I recall a time when I pushed through exhaustion without asking for help, leading to a week of sick leave. After that, I committed to voicing my limits early, which helped me stay healthier and more consistent at work.

Learning to communicate your needs and boundaries effectively is a powerful step toward creating a work life that respects and supports you. It's not always easy, but each conversation builds your confidence and helps shape a more inclusive workplace.

Reflection Questions

1. What are your key communication preferences? How can you share these with your team?
2. What boundaries do you need to set to protect your wellbeing at work?
3. How comfortable are you saying "no" or asking for what you need? What might help you feel more confident?
4. Are there people at work who support your communication? How can you involve them?
5. What small step can you take this week to communicate a need or boundary?

7

Building Positive Workplace Relationships

Workplaces are social environments, and building positive relationships can greatly influence your job satisfaction, productivity and emotional wellbeing. For many autistic people, social interaction can feel complex, unpredictable or draining. But developing meaningful connections at work can also provide support, increase understanding and create a sense of belonging.

Personally, I've found that authentic workplace relationships, built on honesty and respect, are one of the most valuable parts of my career. They don't mean fitting into social norms perfectly; rather, they mean finding ways to connect that feel comfortable and genuine.

Research Insight:

Qualitative work by Bury et al. (2021) shows that when autistic employees encounter unaddressed social challenges - unclear cues, unsupportive colleagues, lack of peer understanding - their stress rises, job satisfaction falls and many report considering leaving their roles.

Socialising at work can be challenging for autistic people. Social cues may be unclear or inconsistent, informal communication styles can feel confusing and sensory issues can make social settings overwhelming.

I remember attending workplace social events where I felt out of sync, unsure whether to join conversations or how to respond. The pressure to "network" or "make small talk" often felt exhausting rather than enjoyable.

Building Connections Your Way

1. Find Your Social Style

There is no one right way to connect with colleagues. Some autistic people thrive in small groups, others prefer one-on-one chats, and some enjoy digital communication more than face-to-face.

For me, I found that sharing written updates on Teams, or joining quiet coffee breaks worked better than large, noisy gatherings. Understanding your social preferences helps you choose environments where you feel most comfortable.

2. Look for Shared Interests

Common interests are natural conversation starters and relationship builders. This could be anything from books and music to hobbies or even shared work goals.

At one job, I bonded with a colleague over a shared love of dogs. That connection opened doors to collaboration and friendship.

3. Be Open About Your Autism (If You Feel Safe)

Disclosing your autism can be a powerful way to build understanding and acceptance. When I started openly sharing my diagnosis with trusted colleagues, I noticed a shift: people became more patient, curious and supportive.

Disclosure is a personal choice. It's okay to keep it private if you're not comfortable or if the environment doesn't feel safe.

4. Use Clear Communication

Social misunderstandings are common, even for neurotypical colleagues. Being clear and direct about your intentions or feelings can prevent confusion.

For example, if you prefer written communication or require breaks during social events, sharing this calmly helps others accommodate your needs.

5. Seek Allies and Mentors

Having at least one trusted person who understands neurodiversity can make a huge difference. Allies can advocate for you, provide advice and help navigate workplace dynamics.

I found a mentor early in my career who became a steady source of support and encouragement.

Navigating Social Misunderstandings

Even with effort, misunderstandings happen. It's a part of human interaction.

When this occurs, I try to:

- Stay calm and clarify my intentions.
- Ask questions to understand the other person's perspective.
- Forgive myself for social mistakes; everyone makes them after all.
- Learn what to do differently next time.

These steps have helped me grow resilience and improved my workplace relationships.

Creating Inclusive Social Spaces

If you're in a position to influence workplace culture, you can help make social spaces more inclusive by:

- Advocating for quieter, low-sensory social events.
- Encouraging clear agendas and expectations for meetings.
- Supporting neurodiversity awareness training for teams.

Together, these changes benefit everyone.

Personal Story: From Isolation to Connection

In one role, I initially felt isolated. Social events were loud and unpredictable, and I often retreated to my desk. Over time, I started inviting a couple of colleagues to quiet lunch breaks and shared my love of art. These small connections blossomed into meaningful friendships that made work feel less lonely and more fulfilling.

Building positive workplace relationships is not about changing who you are; it's about finding ways to connect that honour your unique style and needs. Every small connection adds to your sense of belonging and helps create a workplace culture where neurodiversity is celebrated.

Reflection Questions

1. What kind of social interactions feel comfortable for you at work? How can you create more of these moments?
2. Are there colleagues you feel you can connect with? How might you nurture those relationships?
3. How do you handle social misunderstandings? What strategies help you recover and learn?

4. What boundaries do you need to set to protect your energy during socialising?
5. If you are comfortable, how could sharing your autism with colleagues support better understanding?

8

Organising Your Workday for Focus and Wellbeing

For many autistic people, structure isn't just a preference: it's a necessity. Our brains often thrive with clear routines, predictable rhythms and well-defined tasks. Without these, it's easy to feel overwhelmed, distracted or anxious.

When I first started working full-time, I struggled with unstructured days. Tasks piled up, deadlines snuck up on me, and I felt constantly behind. It wasn't because I wasn't capable, it was because my brain needed a system that fit my way of processing information and managing energy.

A recent systematic review of inclusive workplace practices concludes that flexible accommodations, such as adaptable scheduling, can significantly enhance job integration, diversity, and innovation for neurodivergent employees (Vargas-Salas et al., 2025).

Understanding Your Work Rhythms

Each of us has unique energy patterns throughout the day. Some people are morning larks, others night owls. Many autistic individuals have their own distinctive peaks and troughs in attention and energy.

I learned to notice when I felt most alert, usually first thing, so I scheduled demanding tasks for those times. Less focused periods were for routine or creative thinking tasks.

Understanding your natural rhythms allows you to organise your day to maximise productivity and minimise overwhelm.

Strategies to Structure Your Workday

1. Break Tasks into Manageable Chunks

Big projects can feel daunting. Breaking them into smaller, clear steps makes them easier to start and complete.

For example, instead of "Prepare report", try "Outline main points", "Gather data", "Write introduction", etc.

Task management tools like Asana, Trello or Notion can help to visualise these steps and track progress.

2. Prioritise Tasks

Not everything on your to-do list is equally urgent or important. Use prioritisation methods like the Eisenhower Matrix (urgent vs important) to focus on what truly matters.

I keep a "top three" daily priorities list, which helps me stay focused and feel accomplished.

3. Use Timers and Alarms

Timers can help to stay on task and remind me to take breaks. The Pomodoro Technique is popular and effective: working for 25 minutes, then taking a 5-minute break.

Setting alarms for meetings or deadlines prevents surprises and reduces anxiety.

4. Schedule Sensory and Movement Breaks

Regular breaks aren't just nice, they're necessary. Short walks, stretching or sensory exercises refresh my focus and calm my nervous system.

I often schedule these breaks in my calendar and treat them as important appointments.

5. Minimise Distractions

Open-plan offices, notifications and multitasking can all be major distractions.

I turn off non-essential notifications and use apps to block distracting websites during focused work periods. Noise-cancelling headphones also help.

6. Plan for Transitions

Transitions between tasks or meetings can be challenging. I build in buffer times to mentally switch gears, reducing stress.

For example, scheduling 10 minutes between meetings gives me a moment to regroup.

Using Tools and Technology

There are many tools designed to help organise and manage work:

- Digital calendars: Google Calendar, Outlook
- Task management apps: Trello, Asana, Notion
- Focus tools: Forest app, Focus@Will
- Note-taking: Evernote, OneNote

Experiment with what suits your style and needs. Don't be afraid to customise or combine tools.

Flexibility Within Structure

While routine is important, rigidity can backfire. It's okay, and necessary, to adapt your schedule when unexpected events occur or your energy shifts.

I remind myself that flexibility is part of sustainability. Some days I accomplish less, and that's okay.

Personal Story: Finding My Flow

At one point, I was overwhelmed by juggling multiple projects without clear timelines. After consulting with a mentor, I started breaking tasks into weekly goals and using timers. This approach transformed my productivity and reduced my stress.

Now, I feel more in control and am able to enjoy my work.

Organising your workday is about creating a rhythm that respects your unique brain and body. With patience and experimentation, you can find systems that reduce overwhelm, increase focus and support your wellbeing, helping you succeed both professionally and personally.

Reflection Questions

1. What parts of your current workday structure support your focus and wellbeing? What challenges do you face?
2. When during the day do you feel most and least alert? How can you organise your tasks around these rhythms?
3. Which tools or techniques have you tried or want to try to manage tasks and time?
4. How do you currently take breaks? Could you plan them more intentionally?
5. What small changes could you make to minimise distractions or

transitions?

9

Building Your Career Path on Your Terms

Career paths are rarely linear, especially for autistic people. The traditional idea of climbing a corporate ladder or moving quickly through promotions often doesn't fit our experiences or values. For me, career success has always meant something different; meaningful work aligned with my strengths, autonomy and a respectful environment where I can be myself.

A personalised approach to career development is not only valid but essential. The Buckland Review of Autism Employment (2024) found that 74% of autistic adults would benefit from tailored employment support that reflects their individual strengths, challenges and sensory needs.

What Does Career Growth Look Like?

Growth can mean many things, including:

- Deepening expertise in a specialised area.
- Developing new skills at your own pace.
- Expanding your influence through mentoring or advocacy.

- Shaping roles to better suit your strengths and interests.
- Finding work-life balance that sustains you.

Ask yourself: what feels meaningful and achievable for you?

Identifying Your Strengths and Interests

Understanding your unique talents is the foundation of career building. Many autistic people have exceptional skills, like attention to detail, pattern recognition, creativity or empathy, that can be huge assets.

Reflecting on what energises you and where you excel helps focus your career efforts.

I often turn to my blog reflections where I've tracked moments of flow and accomplishment. These insights guide me toward roles and projects that fit me best.

Navigating Career Conversations

One barrier many autistic employees face is navigating career conversations with managers or HR. These discussions can feel daunting or vague.

Here are some tips I've found helpful:

- Prepare by listing your achievements, strengths and career goals.
- Use clear, specific language about what support or opportunities you want.
- Request regular check-ins to discuss progress and aspirations.
- Bring your own agenda, don't wait for others to initiate.

If possible, ask for a mentor or coach who understands neurodiversity.

You have the right to grow and develop in your job, but sometimes that means advocating for yourself. Whether it's requesting training, shadowing opportunities or flexible projects, being proactive opens doors.

In my experience, framing requests around how your growth benefits the team or organisation helps gain buy-in.

Upskilling on Your Terms

Continuous learning can be empowering but overwhelming if it feels pressured or mismatched.

Choose courses, workshops or reading that genuinely interests you and fits your learning style. Online learning platforms offer flexibility and a wide range of topics.

I prefer bite-sized learning modules I can complete at my own pace, often paired with practical application.

Managing Setbacks and Redefining Goals

Career journeys have ups and downs. Setbacks like rejection, misunderstandings or burnout do not mean failure.

When faced with challenges, I remind myself to:

- Reflect on lessons learned.
- Adjust goals as needed.
- Celebrate small wins.
- Seek support from mentors or peers.

Redefining success to fit your evolving needs is a strength, not a setback.

Personal Story: Finding My Career Path

Early in my career, I pursued roles that didn't align with my strengths, feeling pressured to conform. This led to frustration and burnout.

When I shifted focus to roles that matched my skills in communication and advocacy, and when I advocated for reasonable adjustments, my career blossomed in ways I hadn't imagined.

Building your career on your terms is a journey of self-awareness, advocacy and flexibility. By honouring your unique strengths and values, you create a path that's not only successful, but deeply fulfilling.

Reflection Questions

1. What does career success mean to you personally?
2. What are your key strengths and interests? How can you build on them?
3. How comfortable are you in initiating career conversations? What might help?
4. What opportunities for learning or development excite you?
5. How can you redefine your career goals to fit your needs and wellbeing?

10

Coping with Workplace Challenges

No workplace is perfect, and autistic employees often face unique challenges. Whether it's social misunderstandings, sensory overload, microaggressions or unexpected changes, these hurdles can feel isolating and overwhelming.

Early in my career, I struggled silently with these issues, unsure how to ask for support or manage them effectively. Over time, I learned coping strategies that not only helped me survive difficult moments but also empowered me to prosper.

Common Workplace Challenges for Autistic Employees

- **Social miscommunications:** Subtle cues, implied meanings or unwritten social rules can cause confusion.
- **Sensory overwhelm:** Loud noises, bright lights or crowded spaces trigger overload.
- **Microaggressions and stigma:** Casual remarks or assumptions about autism that hurt or marginalise.
- **Unpredictable changes:** Sudden shifts in tasks, schedules or teams can increase anxiety.

- **Workload and burnout:** Balancing demands without adequate support leads to exhaustion.

Research Insight:

A 2020 scoping review in *Disability and Rehabilitation* found that autistic adults with effective coping strategies and workplace accommodations report significantly less stress and are more likely to remain employed (Khalifa et al., 2020).

Developing Your Personal Coping Toolkit

Here are some approaches that have helped me manage challenges:

1. Take Time-Outs When Needed

If you feel overwhelmed, it's okay to step away briefly. A short walk, a quiet room or deep breathing can reset your nervous system.

I keep a "safe space" in mind at work, a quiet corner or outside area, where I can decompress.

2. Build a Support Network

Having trusted colleagues, mentors or friends who understand your experiences is invaluable. They can offer advice, advocacy or simply a listening ear.

Joining autistic support groups, online or in-person, has also given me a sense of community and shared understanding.

3. Practice Self-Compassion

Challenges can trigger self-criticism. Remember that difficulty is by no means equivalent to failure.

I remind myself regularly that I'm doing my best in a world not always designed for me.

4. Use Clear Communication

If misunderstandings occur, calmly clarifying intentions or asking questions helps resolve conflict and prevent escalation.

5. Know When to Escalate

Sometimes, issues require formal support. Whether it's raising concerns with HR, using grievance procedures or requesting mediation, knowing your rights empowers you.

Managing Specific Challenges

Social Miscommunications

- Use direct questions to clarify meaning.
- Share your communication preferences.
- Prepare responses for common social scenarios.

Sensory Overload

- Use reasonable adjustments like headphones or quiet spaces.
- Plan sensory breaks.
- Communicate sensory needs clearly.

Microaggressions and Stigma

- Decide how and when to respond.
- Seek allies who can support or intervene.
- Use workplace policies on discrimination.

Unexpected Changes

- Ask for advance notice where possible.
- Create backup plans for flexibility.
- Use calming techniques during transitions.

Burnout Prevention

- Track your energy and workload.
- Set realistic boundaries.
- Prioritise rest and self-care.

Personal Story: Learning to Ask for Help

In one role, I struggled silently with sensory overload and miscommunications, leading to burnout. Eventually, I reached out to my manager, explaining my needs and requesting adjustments.

The response was positive, and together we created a plan that included flexible breaks and clearer communication channels. This experience taught me the power of asking for support and the importance of a compassionate workplace.

Workplace challenges are real and sometimes painful, but with the right tools, support and mindset, they can be navigated successfully. Remember, coping is not just about enduring, it's about empowering yourself to create a sustainable, fulfilling work life.

Reflection Questions

1. What workplace challenges have you experienced? How did you respond?
2. Which coping strategies have helped you in difficult moments?
3. Who supports you at work or outside? How can you strengthen this network?
4. Are there situations where you could benefit from formal support? How would you access it?
5. How do you practice self-compassion when challenges arise?

11

Creating a Sustainable Work-Life Balance

Work-life balance isn't just a topical phrase, it's essential for wellbeing, productivity and long-term career success. For autistic people, balancing the demands of work with personal needs can be especially challenging. Our brains may require more downtime to recover from sensory input or social interaction, and traditional expectations around "always on" work cultures can feel overwhelming.

I've learned the hard way that neglecting balance leads to burnout, stress and health issues. Prioritising sustainable rhythms, where work and personal life support rather than compete with each other, is vital.

Research Insight:

Evidence suggests autistic adults are more prone to burnout, marked by profound fatigue, diminished resilience and waning motivation, and that cultivating balance can help mitigate these effects (Hedley et al., 2018). Achieving balance helps protect against this.

Cheak-Zamora and Odunleye (2022) found that autistic young adults experience high levels of stress when juggling new responsibilities in work, education, finances and social relationships. They rely on coping strategies like relaxation exercises, technology distractions and support from friends and family to manage it. Deliberate work–life balance measures, such as embedding regular breaks into the day, offering flexible start and finish times, and clearly separating work tasks from personal time, can build on these individual coping strategies to reduce stress, maintain motivation, and enhance job retention for autistic employees.

Defining What Balance Means to You

Balance looks different for everyone. It's not about perfectly splitting time or energy equally between work and life, but about feeling that both areas meet your needs and values.

For me, balance means having enough time and space to:

- Recharge sensory and emotional energy.
- Engage in passions and hobbies.
- Connect meaningfully with friends and family.
- Manage health and wellbeing proactively.

Strategies for Creating Sustainable Balance

1. Set Clear Boundaries Between Work and Personal Time

This might mean:

- Turning off work emails and notifications outside of work hours.
- Having a dedicated workspace to physically separate work from home life.
- Communicating your availability clearly to colleagues and managers.

I make a rule to avoid checking emails after 5pm unless urgent, which helps me mentally switch off.

2. Plan Rest and Recharge Periods

Downtime isn't lazy, it's restorative. Schedule regular breaks during the workday and plan longer rest periods in your week.

This could include quiet time, sensory-friendly activities, creative rest, mindfulness or just doing nothing.

3. Prioritise Sleep and Nutrition

Good sleep and balanced meals are foundational to energy and focus. Autistic people often experience sleep difficulties, so establishing calming bedtime routines is helpful.

I use heavy blankets, soft toys and calming scents to improve my sleep quality.

4. Delegate and Say No

Protect your energy by learning to say no to non-essential tasks or social events that drain you.

Delegating or asking for help at work can lighten your load and build supportive teamwork.

5. Use Flexible Working Arrangements

Where possible, negotiate flexible hours, remote work or reduced hours.

Flexible schedules allow you to align work with your natural rhythms and personal needs.

6. Engage in Activities That Nourish You

Whether it's creative hobbies, exercise or social time, make space for what fills your cup.

My drawing, nature walks and time with my dog are vital outlets that keep me balanced and grounded.

Overcoming Barriers to Balance

Sometimes workplaces don't support balance; promoting long hours and constant availability or showing a lack of understanding.

Advocate for yourself by:

- Requesting reasonable adjustments related to workload or schedule.
- Sharing your needs with your manager or HR.
- Connecting with employee wellbeing programs.

Personal Story: Reclaiming My Evenings

For a while, I answered emails late into the night, convinced it was necessary to prove my dedication. This routine drained me physically and emotionally.

Once I committed to shutting down work devices by a set time, my stress levels dropped, sleep improved, and I felt more present in my life outside work.

Creating sustainable work-life balance is a journey of tuning into your needs, setting boundaries and honouring your wellbeing. By doing so, you not only enhance your professional life but nurture your whole self, allowing you to thrive long term.

Reflection Questions

1. What does work-life balance look like for you personally?
2. What boundaries can you set to protect your personal time?
3. How do you currently recharge outside work? What new activities might help?
4. Are there workplace adjustments or support you could request to improve balance?

5. How can you practice self-compassion when balance feels out of reach?

12

Conclusion

Thank you for taking this journey with me through *The Autism Employee Workplace Toolkit.* I hope this book has offered you practical strategies, compassion and encouragement to navigate your work life with confidence and authenticity.

Being autistic in the workplace brings unique challenges, but also incredible strengths and perspectives that enrich any team and organisation. You deserve to be seen, supported and celebrated for who you are.

Remember: thriving at work is not about fitting into a mould, but about shaping your environment and career to fit around you. It's about self-advocacy, setting boundaries, managing sensory and emotional wellbeing, building connections, and organising your day in ways that honour your needs.

This toolkit is just the beginning. Keep learning, keep reaching out and keep believing in your worth. You are not alone, and your success matters.

If you want to continue the conversation, explore more insights, or connect with me, visit my blog at www.mahliaamatina.com/workplace-blog. Together, we can change workplaces for the better, one step at a time.

13

Bibliography

Austin, R. D., & Pisano, G. P. (2017). Neurodiversity as a competitive advantage. *Harvard Business Review.* https://hbr.org/2017/05/neurodiversity-as-a-competitive-advantage

Bury, S.M., Flower, R.L., Zulla, R. et al. Workplace Social Challenges Experienced by Employees on the Autism Spectrum: An International Exploratory Study Examining Employee and Supervisor Perspectives. J Autism Dev Disord 51, 1614–1627 (2021). https://doi.org/10.1007/s10803-020-04662-6

Centre for Inclusive Employment. (2023). *Closing the Fair Work Gap: Making Work Fair for Autistic People.* Into Work. https://intowork.org.uk/wp-content/uploads/2023/11/Closing-the-Fair-Work-Gap-Summary-Report.pdf

Cheak-Zamora, N. L., & Odunleye, O. (2022). Stress and coping in autistic young adults. Autism in Adulthood, 4(3). https://doi.org/10.1089/aut.2021.0043

Davies, Jade & Heasman, Brett & Livesey, Adam & Walker, Amy & Pellicano, Elizabeth & Remington, Anna. (2022). Autistic adults' views and experiences of requesting and receiving workplace adjustments in the UK. PLOS ONE. 17. e0272420. 10.1371/journal.pone.0272420

Department for Work and Pensions. (2024). *The Buckland Review of Autism Employment: Report and Recommendations.* Supported by Autistica. https://www.gov.uk/government/publications/the-buckland-review-of-autism-employment-report-and-recommendations

Equality Act 2010, c. 15. (Great Britain). https://www.legislation.gov.uk/ukpga/2010/15/contents

Equality and Human Rights Commission. (n.d.). *Your rights under the Equality Act 2010.* https://www.equalityhumanrights.com/

Goldfarb, Y., Golan, O., & Gal, E. (2023). A Self-Determination Theory Approach to Work Motivation of Autistic Adults: A Qualitative Exploratory Study. *Journal of Autism and Developmental Disorders*, 53, 1529–1542. https://doi.org/10.1007/s10803-021-05185-4

Hedley D, Uljarević M, Foley KR, Richdale A, Trollor J. Risk and protective factors underlying depression and suicidal ideation in Autism Spectrum Disorder. *Depress Anxiety.* 2018 Jul;35(7):648-657. doi: 10.1002/da.22759. Epub 2018 Apr 16. PMID: 29659141

Khalifa, G., Sharif, Z., Sultan, M., & Di Rezze, B. (2020). *Workplace accommodations for adults with autism spectrum disorder: A scoping review. Disability and Rehabilitation*, 42(9), 1316–1331. https://doi.org/10.1080/09638288.2018.1527952

MacLennan, K., O'Brien, S., & Tavassoli, T. (2021). *In Our Own Words: The Complex Sensory Experiences of Autistic Adults. Autism Research*, 14(10), 2187–2199. https://doi.org/10.1002/aur.2554

McKinsey & Company. (2020). *Diversity wins: How inclusion matters.* https://www.mckinsey.com/business-functions/organization/our-insights/diversity-wins-how-inclusion-matters

National Autism Indicators Report. (n.d.). *Transition into young adulthood.* Drexel University Autism Institute. https://drexel.edu/autismoutcomes/publications-and-reports/national-autism-indicators-report/

National Autistic Society (2016). *The Autism Employment Gap.*

https://www.autism.org.uk/what-we-do/news/government-must-tackle-the-autism-employment-gap

Office for National Statistics. (2021). *Outcomes for disabled people in the UK: 2021.* https://www.ons.gov.uk/peoplepopulationandcommunity/healthandsocialcare/disability/articles/outcomesfordisabledpeopleintheuk/2021

Pearson, A., & Rose, K. (2021). A conceptual analysis of autistic masking: Understanding the narrative of stigma and the illusion of choice. *Autism in Adulthood*, 3(1), 52–60. https://www.liebertpub.com/doi/10.1089/aut.2020.0043

Petty, S., Tunstall, L., Richardson, H., & Eccles, N. (2022). *Workplace Adjustments for Autistic Employees: What is 'Reasonable'? Journal of Autism and Developmental Disorders*, 53(1), 236–244. https://doi.org/10.1007/s10803-021-05413-x

Pincus, J. D., & Beller, K. (2025). Emotional wellbeing in neurodivergent populations. Frontiers in Psychology, 16, 1606232. https://doi.org/10.3389/fpsyg.2025.1606232

Praslova, L. N. (2024). How to weigh the risks of disclosing a disability. *Harvard Business Review.* https://hbr.org/2024/05/how-to-weigh-the-risks-of-disclosing-a-disability

Raymaker, D. M., Teo, A. R., Steckler, N. A., Lentz, B., Scharer, M., Delos Santos, A., ... & Nicolaidis, C. (2020). "Having all of your internal resources exhausted beyond measure and being left with no clean-up crew": Defining autistic burnout. *Autism in Adulthood*, 2(2), 132–143. https://doi.org/10.1089/aut.2019.0079

Vargas-Salas O, Alcazar-Gonzales JC, Fernández-Fernández FA, Molina-Rodríguez FN, Paredes-Velazco R, Carcausto-Zea ML. Neurodivergence and the Workplace: A Systematic Review of the Literature. *Journal of Vocational Rehabilitation.* 2025;63(1):83-94. doi:10.1177/10522263251337564

About the Author

Mahlia Amatina is an award-winning neurodivergent author, artist and advocate, passionate about creativity, inclusion and reimagining the workplace. Diagnosed as autistic in adulthood and named one of the *Top 50 Influential Neurodiverse Women*, by Women Beyond the Box, Mahlia brings both lived experience and professional insight to her work, bridging the gap between theory, research and the day-to-day realities of autistic life.

Join Mahlia's online community and never miss a new project:

You can connect with me on:

- https://www.mahliaamatina.com
- https://www.mahliaamatina.com
- https://www.mahliaamatina.com
- https://www.instagram.com/MahliaAmatina

Also by Mahlia Amatina

If this book spoke to you, please take a moment to leave a review:

- On your reading platform
- On Goodreads, search "Mahlia Amatina" to find her author page
- Directly on Mahlia's website via the contact form

Your feedback helps Mahlia reach more readers and continue advocating for inclusivity within the workplace. Thank you!

Autism and Work

Thriving in the Workplace is a supportive, practical guide by autistic artist and advocate Mahlia Amatina. Blending lived experience with empowering advice, it offers strategies to help you understand your strengths, advocate for your needs and build a fulfilling work life. Whether you're newly diagnosed or years into your journey, this book reminds you: you belong.

Dear Manager: How to Support Your Autistic Employees

Unlock the potential of autistic talent - and transform your workplace.

Written by an autistic professional, *Dear Manager: How to Support Your Autistic Employees* blends lived experience, cutting-edge research and practical strategies to help managers and HR teams create truly inclusive environments. Covering everything from reasonable adjustments and sensory needs to the role of intersectionality in shaping experiences, this is your essential guide to helping autistic employees not just survive, but thrive.

Creative Rest: An Artful Toolkit for Autistic Overwhelm

Gentle exercises and heartfelt guidance to help you find peace, clarity and joy through creativity.

In a world that rarely slows down, autistic minds often carry the weight of sensory overload, social pressure and emotional intensity. Rest can feel unreachable or misunderstood. This book invites you to discover a different kind of rest: one that's creative, compassionate and deeply healing.

Through accessible art exercises, reflective journalling prompts and nurturing self-care strategies, *Creative Rest* offers a gentle path back to yourself. Whether you're navigating overwhelm, shutdown or emotional fatigue, this toolkit will help you regulate your feelings, reconnect with your inner world and honour your unique needs with kindness.

There is no "right" way to rest creatively: only your way. This book is your safe space to explore, express and renew at your own pace, reminding you that rest isn't a luxury but a vital act of self-love.

Autistic Burnout and Mental Health at Work

Feeling drained, overwhelmed or on the edge of burnout? For autistic professionals, burnout isn't just stress: it's survival.

In *Autistic Burnout & Mental Health at Work*, Mahlia Amatina combines lived experience, research and practical tools to help you:

Recognise the early signs of autistic burnout

Recover with phased returns, sensory restoration and energy pacing

Request reasonable adjustments and Access to Work support

Build sustainable wellbeing and belonging at work

Whether you're autistic, supporting an autistic colleague or creating an inclusive workplace, this book offers clarity, compassion and strategies you can use right away.

You are not broken. You are worthy of rest, support and a working life that lets you thrive.

www.ingramcontent.com/pod-product-compliance
Lightning Source LLC
LaVergne TN
LVHW090333210926
848480LV00004B/1391
9781919553887